Advance Praise for The True Marriage...

"I have given your book, The True Marriage, to some friends and I'm giving copies to my three married sons for Christmas. It's a wonderful book, and a great helper."
— **JACQUES ALLEMBERT, Vermont, USA**

"...this book is very thoughtful and wise; in fact, it matches some of my own longings to discover wisdom that moves beyond communication skills in marriage therapy."
— **SALLY RUSSO, former Clinical Director of Psychiatric Social Services, Institute of Pennsylvania Hospital**

"...I read your lovely little book, The True Marriage, last evening. You certainly hit the proverbial nail on the head. I especially resonate with the need for patience, compassion and love. This book would be perfect for marriage counselors to 'read' with their clients. It is gentle and probing rather than commandment-directed."
— **ROY FAIRFIELD, Professor Emeritus, The Union Institute**

"Dr. Rush's unique perspective is based on insights gained through years of experience and compassionate engagement in the real-life struggles of people in marriage."
— **JONATHAN GRANOFF, Esq., President, Global Security Institute**

"I read this book on the weekend and loved it…it's all about love, isn't it…how we treat our partner…how we say things…timing…being patient…being loving."
— **BARBARA KLEIN, Regional Director of Sales and Group Development, SRS-WorldHotels**

"I just recently read the book three times in one day I enjoyed it so much. I am excited and making changes daily in my relationship, which are already beginning to create a healthier and more loving relationship than I have had in over six years."
— **MINDY FONTAINE, Schoolteacher, Steamboat Springs, Colorado, USA**

"A wonderful book that recognizes that marriage is work. In this day of quick fixes and 'who is to blame for my problems?,' this look at marriage holds partners accountable for making the marriage come first, not the individual."
— **TANIA COFFEY, Colorado, USA**

The author shares with us his reflections on marriage and his wisdom about living based on his own experiences and his study of Sufi and Christian mystics. He sees marriage as an opportunity for a special kind of spiritual communication and a challenge for self-development. Thoughtful. Provocative.
— **WINTHROP R. ADKINS PhD, Professor Emeritus of Psychology and Education, Teachers College, Columbia University**

The True Marriage

Locke Rush, Ph.D.

For further information, visit the website at
www.thetruemarriage.com

Copyright ©2003 by Locke Rush, Ph.D.

ISBN 0-9726607-0-4

Printed in the United States of America

Acknowledgments

Much love to my wife, Jackie,
for enriching my life in so many ways and
for encouraging me in this work.
Without her there would be no book.

Appreciation and thanks to my editor,
Sarah Aschenbach of Inspired Solutions, whose
creative talent in structuring and editing contributed
so strongly to the final form of this book.

Appreciation and thanks, also, to
Larry Didona of Didona Design for his fine
layout and cover treatment.

With deepest gratitude and love to
M. R. Bawa Muhaiyaddeen,
(God's peace and blessings be upon him)
without whose wisdom and compassion
I would still be searching.

The True Marriage

The true marriage is a revelation of the meaning of our lives,
a vehicle that can carry us closer to God
than we had ever imagined.
The true marriage is a revolt against all modern reason,
against all techniques and apologia for expanding our egos.
The true marriage subdues the ego, psychology enhances it.
The true marriage is a great task that requires understanding,
vision, motivation, surrender, dedication and, above all,
faith that This Is The Way.
The true marriage says
It's not what is given us that matters,
but how we deal with it,
for only in dealing with anger, frustration, loneliness and despair
can we build the vehicle that can carry us to our destination,
the vehicle built of God's qualities.
The true marriage keeps us on the razor's edge.
If we slip to one side we become lazy,
to the other we become angry,
but balanced on that edge,
we walk the difficult yet wonderful path to God.

Table of Contents

༺

Introduction

When I was thirty years old, I left the United States and went abroad as part of a spiritual search. I wanted to find God and to find true peace. In the process, I wanted to understand myself. Many different religions tell us that if we can come to know ourselves and our own true nature, we can know God. Ten years later, I returned home having undergone many experiences, including a year in a Japanese Zen monastery. I had learned a lot about the world but little about myself.

Not long afterward, I met the only true wise man I have ever encountered, a tiny and very old man with a white beard and eyes that saw into my heart. This was the great Sufi Master M.R. Bawa Muhaiyaddeen. Bawa showed me that the qualities of God exist within us and that it is through these qualities that we can know ourselves and find true peace. Reaching them is difficult, however, because these Godly qualities are obscured by the darker side of our nature: layers of karma, the ego, the monkey mind, desire, arrogance and torpor, which block our progress to the inner heart.

Although I could understand this intellectually, I still wasn't changing or becoming a better human being. I lived alone, which made it easy for me to unconsciously circumvent the arrogant side of my personality. I could put on a very good act. I succeeded in fooling myself and others because there was no work that made me face my darker side.

Then I got married, and everything changed. I learned more about myself in the first year of marriage than I did during my year in the Zen monastery. A few more years into the marriage, my wife and I were arguing and fighting regularly. Something was very wrong, and I was convinced my wife was the problem. I wrote out a list of all her faults. I was certain that our marriage would be just fine if only she would get rid of these faults.

During this time in our lives, I went on a spiritual retreat to Sri Lanka to be with Bawa. One afternoon while I was sitting in Bawa's room, he looked at me and said quietly, "My child, you wrote the wrong list. You should have written down all of your own faults instead of your wife's."

These words made a powerful impact on me, especially since I had never mentioned my list of grievances!

When I returned home several months later, I began to change the way I acted toward my wife. I gave up criticizing her faults and set about correcting my own. Almost immediately, my resentments, my arrogance toward her and my self-pity seemed to vanish.

A year or so later, I came across that old list of my wife's faults. Miraculously, each issue had been resolved. Our marriage was better than it had ever been. Marriage is a mirror, a reflection of all our faults. We cannot fool our partner for long. The wise individual will seize the opportunity that marriage presents to see himself with clarity and find true inner peace. Bawa taught me that spiritual progress comes only through the internal struggle between our good qualities and our bad ones, and there is no experience that I know more suited to provoke and intensify this struggle than marriage. To find true peace, we have to come to grips with our arrogance, anger and impatience. We cannot go around them; we have to conquer them. Spiritual progress involves an internal war, a holy war.

In my therapy practice, I have counseled many couples. Most couples genuinely want peace, but they are searching for it in the wrong place. Usually, both people feel that a satisfying and peaceful marriage would be attainable if only their partner would change. They strive in vain to change the world around them. Very few truly understand that the only path to peace is to conquer and subdue their own bad habits. And of the few who understand this, even fewer are actually willing to "walk the walk," to work on themselves and to learn true surrender and humility.

It is for those who truly want peace and cannot understand why marriage is so difficult that I decided to write this book. Everything we are given in this life is either a duty or a lesson, and marriage is both of these. In my own marriage, I have slowly come to understand that progress requires faith and certitude and a spiritual base. Progress is slow, but with effort, the demands of marriage will bring about a true transformation. I know of no other arena that will offer this transformation as dramatically as marriage. We help ourselves, we help our partner and we serve God.

May God grace us all in our lives. May He grant us the wisdom and patience to understand this wondrous thing we call marriage.

Why We Marry

⊚❦⊚

Why do we marry? We marry to have children, to enjoy companionship, to share the burdens of life with someone else. We marry because of societal demands, parental pressure, tradition. There are a thousand reasons why people choose to marry. Once we decide, we take marriage vows, for better or for worse, for richer for poorer, in sickness and in health, till death do us part, amen. We begin well-intentioned, enthusiastic and eager to move forward in our new life together, but the honeymoon ends sooner than expected for most of us. A few years into marriage everything is going wrong. Romance has been replaced by demands, necessities and ingrained routines that gradually erode earlier good intentions. Duty, responsibility and self-abnegation have eclipsed the romantic beginnings.

There may be little peace in the home. Often, communications have deteriorated into name-calling or cynicism or resentful tolerance. Two young people who seemed so good for each other have arrived at a major impasse. At this point, many marriages deteriorate and divorce occurs. Over fifty percent of marriages in the United States today end in divorce.

We all react to these changes differently. Some of us accept them gracefully, others resist them strongly, and some of us choose to end our marriages. But all of us, at one time or another, have questioned our marriages. Is this what marriage is supposed to be? Where is the person I married? I still see the good qualities, but many bad ones have surfaced. Why should I have to put up with these difficulties? Why did I marry? What is the point of it beyond having someone to help keep a house or raise children? Wouldn't I be better off single again? At least I wouldn't have these aggravations, these intrusions into my way of doing things. Are there secrets about marriage I don't understand? Is there any spiritual significance to what I am going through? Something in me tells me this way of life is good and worthwhile, but why should it involve all these problems?

Let us explore some of these questions and try to understand our marriages and ourselves. If we can understand our situations psychologically and spiritually, we may experience less confusion and even discover the true value of marriage on our journey through life.

Stages of Marriage

Romance
Disillusionment
Misery
Enlightenment
Love

—AUTHOR UNKNOWN

Getting What We Want
Is the Wrong Peace

What has taken place before a person walks down the aisle? What do we bring to this union? What is the mind-set of people entering marriage? In essence, why are we the way we are? What has conditioned us and how?

We are all alike in one sense. We all want the same thing—peace. Most of us never find it because we are looking for it in the wrong place. Free will is for many the *summum bonnum*. If we can do what we want, we think this will guarantee happiness. The idea seems to be that happiness is a gold ring to grab as we go round and round on the carousel of life.

We have been conditioned to win. We are taught from an early age that winning is a great thing. Just watch parents at a little league contest! And look at our society today with the enormous importance placed on winning and gaining control. Vince Lombardi, the great NFL football coach said, "Winning isn't everything—it's the only thing!" We often take this saying to heart, as if it were a heavenly pronouncement. Rarely does a day pass in the average household that the husband isn't glued to the TV, savoring the triumph or cursing the defeat of his favorite team. Elated investors watch their stock rise as a big company takes over a smaller company.

The extent to which we go to insure our rights, our privileges and our wants is amazing. Anything that interferes with or threatens our way of life is the enemy and must be dispensed with quickly. Look at what happens on the highway. People drive like maniacs, determined to stay at the head of the pack. At the same time, a person who disrespects another's rights in traffic may be in for a frightening encounter. People have even been shot and killed for violating another driver's space. Observe also the recent rash of teenage mothers disposing of their newborns in trash bins. Our egos have been inflated and indulged to an extreme.

Children naturally want to get their way, so their parents curb them and set limits. As they approach adolescence, children who previously had no power and no ability to determine their own lives begin to sense new strengths, even the ability to procreate. Children test these new strengths and all the boundaries that have been set up by their parents. They yearn for autonomy and begin to stretch parental boundaries to the breaking point. Free will exerts itself and constantly repeats the mantra, "This is my right. I can do what I please. Don't interfere with me."

This attitude metamorphoses gradually into ego, and ego tends to expand, solidifying its gains much like an advancing army.

Out of this cauldron of urges and rebellion comes the average young adult who one day decides to get married. Many young adults are woefully unfit for marriage. They have become accustomed through their upbringing or lack of it to getting their own way. They have seen little or no tolerance or compassion in their families of origin. Their driving motivation is to escape pain and experience pleasure. "Life owes me a living. Look what it's done to me." Seeking and experiencing pleasure has subtly and gradually replaced seeking and practicing goodness.

To one degree or another, this is the mind-set most of us bring into marriage. We are flying free, young adults who have broken out of the cocoon of parental conditioning and influence. We cherish our new freedoms, and we are eager to perpetuate and strengthen them. We are flying, and we value highly our right to fly where we will, stop where we will and do as we please.

Marriage changes things. It is the exact opposite of flying free because both people have to compromise their way of behaving and even their convictions. In other words, the real struggle is with ourselves, not with our partner. We cannot change anyone else. The only war worth fighting takes place in the battlefield of the heart.

You have probably heard the Arabic word *jihad* in the news. It is also and probably more commonly called holy war. Even in Islamic countries, *jihad* is usually taken to mean a war of believer against infidel. The true meaning of this word has been forgotten. *Jihad* does indeed mean war, but in the Q'uran, *jihad* was used to refer to the war that is fought inside the heart, the war of good qualities against bad qualities.

What does this mean?

I have talked about how our conditioning affects our marriages, specifically the extreme focus on winning and getting our own way. Another important aspect of our conditioning has to do with childhood experiences of abandonment, rejection and blame. Such experiences are universal because most parents are unskilled and, what is more, most are struggling with their own childhood wounds while they are raising their children. Deep inside, we carry resentments and even anger because of parental neglect or abuse, but we are largely unaware of these feelings and how they are affecting our marriages and our lives.

Increasingly these days, we turn to various therapies for help. Therapists point out these underlying feelings. We learn how our early conditioning has affected us. We uncover child abuse, abandonment, suppressed anger, and so forth. Too often, we come to derive a certain sense of comfort about our negative conditioning. We may use it as an excuse. "Of course

I have trouble dealing with people and life! Look at the awful things that have happened to me."

In reality, equal to our conditioning, if not far more important, is the fact that genetically we carry all the good and bad traits that must be worked out to achieve peace in life. These good and bad traits are the two sides of our nature. It is crucial to remember, however, that we should never feel guilty about having negative traits. They are an inevitable part of the human condition, and we should strive to view them as objectively as possible. I feel that I must emphasize this point because so many couples I have counseled are guilt-ridden, which is absolutely useless.

Our physical constitution is made of five elements, the elements of the world: earth, fire, water, air and ether. Each element spawns specific base desires in the human being. Fire, for example, begets anger. The base desires are part of our human nature, and they become manifest in our thoughts and actions as anger, arrogance, greed, lust, deceit, cruelty and impatience, to name only a few.

These negative qualities are inherent; we were born with them and we cannot escape them, no matter how noble our lineage, how fine our parents or how skillfully we were parented. Because we are not aware of this, we tend to blame all of our present misery on either our marriage partner or our negative childhood experiences or both. It is true, of course, that some of these developmental and environmental factors contribute to our problems, but they are not the primary cause — *the elements out of which we are formed are the primary source of our unhappiness.*

Since we cannot escape them, how can we deal with these elements and the fundamental desires connected with them? Here we come to the other side of our dual nature. God in all His wisdom provided antidotes, neutralizers, erasers to help us cope with the destructive forces that are part of our animal nature. These antidotes are known as the beautiful qualities of God. There are many Godly qualities, among them patience, tolerance, forgiveness, compassion, wisdom, surrender, understanding and conscience. These Godly qualities, which are also inherent in our nature, are the only effective tools for coping with the darker side of our nature (our negative genetic or karmic predisposition).

This is an extremely important understanding. We will never find happiness if we go through life blaming our discontent on the world, on our marriage partners, on what is being done to us or on what has been done to us. If, on the other hand, we identify the dark qualities inside of us that generate discontent as the true villains, it will be possible to find a way out of our dilemma if we choose to do so. As the saying goes, in the darkness we have a choice: we can either curse the darkness or light a light.

The difficult part is clearing away or neutralizing the base desires so that we can see the Godly side of our nature.

Much misery in life could be averted if parents would teach their children about these elements and why and how we must control them. Ideally, our upbringing instills in us the value of morality, but focus on God and virtue is becoming increasingly rare. In olden days, children were taught to love and respect God. They were encouraged to believe that He is always here watching and responding to our prayers. This message is rarely given more than lip service today, and sometimes not even that. Oh, we may turn to God in moments of despair and grief or in fear of our lives, but daily practice of remembrance of God and the practice of good qualities is fairly rare.

I am reminded of a story I heard once. A small boy was fascinated by the newborn in his family. One day, when the boy thought he was alone with the infant, he leaned over the cradle and said softly, "Tell me what God is like. I've almost forgotten." Consciousness of God is natural to the newborn infant, but it fades quickly into the far background as our conditioning takes hold.

If we accept marriage as an excellent vehicle for spiritual progress, we have already made a big step, for we will then begin to see everything differently. We will not take things so personally—instead we will be aware that marriage is a barometer of our inner struggle, a call to our own *jihad*. For it is a *jihad*; true marriage involves intense, quiet inner warfare — good against bad, good qualities as opposed to bad ones — a true spiritual exercise.

Most people, however, certainly do take the trials of marriage very personally. When marriage is not seen for its potential or spiritual significance, it quickly lapses into a struggle between two people, one that is bound to produce frustration and despair. A power struggle emerges, and winning becomes paramount. The battle must be won; surrender is unthinkable. And yet, while winning the battle we may end up losing the war. Letting go and surrendering may mean losing the battle, but it also may mean winning the war to save the marriage. So often, gracious surrender brings about the most unexpected results. In my own marriage, my wife's acts of kindness and surrender have been far more healing than fighting to see who wins.

Marriage is not a problem to be solved but a challenge to be accepted and understood as an opportunity for our own growth. Marriage shows us the areas we need to perfect in ourselves.

We Can Only Change Ourselves

The most important thing to remember is that we cannot change our partner; we can only change ourselves. No marriage succeeds without this understanding. In *The Alchemy of Happiness*, Al Ghazzali, one of the great mystic writers of the Middle Ages, states, "Man has a lower nature, and, till he can control his own lower nature, he had better not assume the responsibility of controlling another's."

Our resistance to change, however, is very strong. "I'm not the one who needs to change," we mutter to ourselves.

There is a saying: "When God goes, I am there; when I go, God is there." The 'I' is the ego, the base desires, the negative qualities, the arrogance which maintains that there are two ways—the wrong way and my way.

For real change to occur, we have to get back to some fundamental questions: Why am I here in this world? What is the purpose for which I was born? What part does marriage play in life here on earth?

Nothing changed in my own marriage until I had

answered these questions. What I discovered is that we are born to understand and experience our true nature so that we can progress, pass our exams and go on to our rightful place after death. This task can only be accomplished or worked on while we are here in this world. Our very existence on earth, the reason we are here, is to recognize and understand who we really are.

I discovered that the true self or soul is occluded by the mind's desires. Much as a pure metal can only be obtained by the smelting process, this physical world provides a large furnace for clearing away the impurities of our being. If we can clear ourselves, we will see our true nature and understand the reason for our birth and our struggle in this life.

There are many different catalysts in our lives to facilitate this process, but by far the greatest of these is marriage. Marriage is the great furnace, the great purifier, the character builder.

As I mentioned earlier, I spent a year in a Zen Monastery in Japan and several more years there pursuing a monastic, meditative existence, seeking spiritual knowledge. Even so, I learned more about myself in my first year of marriage than in all that time. Why? No institution or experience besides marriage provides a clearer mirror. In marriage, reflected back to us with startling clarity when we dare to look, we see ourselves: our ugliness, our defects, our good nature and our potential. We can fool anyone except the person to whom we are married. If we truly want to become better human beings or, better yet, enlightened human beings, marriage is a direct path, albeit a steep and difficult one.

Peace is something we have to earn. To earn it means going through and not around the difficulty. It means dealing with one's ego—one's own way of doing things. Marriage is difficult because it involves, on the outside, surrender to another's will and, on the inside, surrender of our vanity and pride to tolerance. Marriage requires real work.

If a husband and wife
can control impatience and anger,
they will become as suited to one another
as a flower and its fragrance,
living in harmony and without
ever separating.

A husband and wife who reflect on this
will mingle in the way
the fragrance mingles with a flower.
This will give them victory in their lives.

—M. R. BAWA MUHAIYADDEEN

The Gap

During courtship, people tend to present themselves in as good a light as possible. It is easy to see each other's goodness, because both people are working to show it.

Once again, marriage changes things. No longer do we need to sell ourselves — the prize has been won. As time goes on, however, it is easy to forget how very appealing the good qualities of our partners were. And, when we ignore the good qualities and see only the faults, it hurts the marriage. If, however, we can remember how strong certain qualities were, like strength or thoughtfulness, our marriages will improve. The gifts that attracted us have not disappeared. We have simply overlooked them, taken them for granted. We need to search for them in our partner and remind ourselves of just how good our partner is.

Much of the misery that occurs in a marriage arises from what I call 'the gap.' The gap is the space between how we think our partners should be and how they actually are in daily life. If we have a picture in our minds of how our partners should believe, act, talk and think, then every time they say or do anything that doesn't measure up to these levels, we note the discrepancy and point it out. Our complaints mount. "I should be getting ninety percent from my partner and I'm only getting sixty-five percent. How can I be so deprived? I don't deserve this." This tendency to judge, left unchecked, can and will develop into the worst-case scenario: 'the grass is greener' syndrome. Once this occurs, the marriage is doomed to a slow death.

How often in an unhappy marriage filled with unrequited love and spiritual bankruptcy does a partner seek solace or companionship elsewhere? Sometimes it is benign and useful, as with a friend of the same sex. More often than not, however, as the gap widens we may seek the answer to our problems in Mister or Miss Wonderful, who seems to embody all the qualities our partner lacks. The new confidant rarely loses in a comparison contest. He or she is not the one who has to bear the responsibilities of the family, the pressures of child raising or the economics of the home. These confidants can do no wrong. They are seen as the panacea to the life of the disgruntled partner, and the more involved or enmeshed the married person becomes, the more the marriage deteriorates.

When infidelity or other serious difficulties have

developed, couples may seek counseling, hoping to clarify their situation and find a way to resolve differences. Unfortunately, the marriage counselor may be unable to lead a couple out of their difficulty because he or she has the same unresolved problems! But there is also another reason. If a marriage is in deep trouble, book psychology will not suffice. It just doesn't work. It has its place, of course. Most marriage counseling done today is well-intentioned. It works with behavior modification tools and understanding of codependency issues. The counselor can point out the personality defects of each partner, codependent patterns, effects of childhood abuse or neglect, and any other affective disorders influencing the couple. So far so good. But analyzing and understanding problems is only a small portion of the solution. In extreme cases, people spend years in psychoanalysis to find out why they do the things they do. If indeed they discover some answers, the understanding gained usually is not sufficient to change the behavior.

I remember a well-known psychiatrist in New York City, an older gentleman who lived on Park Avenue. He told me of a patient, a wealthy woman who loved the arts and devoted her life to them. Every night she attended a different concert, opera, ballet or theater performance. The only problem was that she had to have an aisle seat because she became claustrophobic if she sat even one seat in from the aisle.

After several years of analysis, the psychiatrist discovered the cause. As a child she had accidentally locked herself in a closet when her parents were out of the house, and she was trapped in the closet for several hours. The experience had deeply scarred her, so much so that she always had to have an escape route open and nothing to block it.

When the woman discovered the 'cause' of her problem, she was ecstatic. She thanked the doctor profusely and went on her way. A year later the psychiatrist told me he saw her sitting in front of him at the opera—in an aisle seat. He told me this story with a twinkle in his eye. So much for knowing why we do something or fear something; the knowledge in itself is not enough to change us or our behavior.

If we keep things at a psychological or behavioral level, we may never change. "Why should I change?" we ask ourselves. "I like myself the way I am. What's in it for me if I change?" and eventually, "How do I change?"

The answer to these questions lies at a higher level. To change one's self requires real motivation. Sometimes we grow to accept and even like our misery. Some people feel entitled to their anger; it is their 'right.' They may even enjoy exercising their right to be angry.

Both partners may want a good marriage, but both also may want to cling to their old behavior patterns.

When real infighting exists in a marriage, when we are dealing with stored hostilities, codependency issues, self-justifications and blame, it is very difficult to envision changing ourselves. It is all too easy to blame the partner. If both people fall into this trap, there is gridlock. What truth or conviction is powerful enough to lift someone out of this predicament, enabling serious self-work to begin?

Sow a thought, reap an action.
Sow an action, reap a habit.
Sow a habit, reap a character.
Sow a character, reap a destiny.

—AUTHOR UNKNOWN

The Goal, The Work

We tend to forget that marriage involves three entities: the husband, the wife and the marriage. If husband and wife don't acknowledge the third party and nourish it, if they don't put some work into it, there is no growth. Like anything worthwhile, marriage requires attention and effort.

If you want to create a bountiful garden, you have to work at it. You have to prepare the ground, dig out the rocks, break up the clumps of dirt, till the soil, plant seeds, fertilize and add mulch and compost. Then for a few months you have to water, weed, spray and prune. If you focus on your goal, your work will produce a beautiful harvest of fruits and vegetables.

A gemologist who wants to create a valuable gem must examine the rough stone thoroughly, cut it with minute care to preserve its character and spend a long time faceting it and polishing it. His focus on his work produces a gemstone of enormous beauty and value.

A mechanic who is intent on restoring an automobile to tip-top shape has to take the engine apart and build it back up lovingly, cleaning and oiling each part. When he finds a faulty part, he fixes it or replaces it. Once the engine has been rebuilt, he examines it carefully. Finally, he takes a test drive to see how the automobile performs. The engine sings its song, and the mechanic is pleased. His focus on his work produces a finely-tuned, well-running machine that is both functional and aesthetic.

The same is true when it comes to developing a good marriage. If we want to have a good marriage, we must focus on it and understand that work and frustration are part of achieving that goal. Marriage is not something to start and stop—or something to leave when it is difficult. Gardeners don't give up halfway through and then blame the plants for not growing. Gemologists and mechanics don't stop working until they have achieved their goals. Yet look at marriages today: remember, half of them end in divorce. The partners have no tolerance for difficulties, and divorce is seen as the only solution.

What has happened to the goal? What has happened to the intention necessary to reach it? We cannot attain the goal without working toward it. Increasingly these days, this fact is forgotten when it comes to marriage.

True marriage exists when two people become one and journey together as one. When they travel by sea, the husband must be the boat and the wife must be the one who steers. When they climb a mountain, the wife must be the walking stick and the husband the climber. When they cross the desert, one must be the camel and the other the rider. Sometimes the positions will have to be reversed. That is what married life is like.

—M. R. BAWA MUHAIYADDEEN

Communication, Intimacy & Trust

The First Intimacy

We have talked of the roots of ego and its base desires as part of our fundamental nature. These desires are strengthened by another factor mentioned earlier — our conditioning.

The most common complaint in marriage is lack of communication, which is a key factor in drifting toward divorce. Most couples put poor communication first on their list of grievances. There are two aspects to this problem, the first more obvious than the second.

First, both parties become more and more set in their ways. Each is used to doing things in his or her own way and resents the very idea of changing. As the marriage continues, habitual ways of speaking and acting harden. Laziness, habit, arrogance, resentment — all tend to reinforce our lack of response. Conscious effort is required to undo these fixed habits. Understanding, tolerance and compassion must be practiced daily to develop honest communication.

The second aspect of communication is more subtle and difficult to correct—intimacy. Why is this area so threatening? Why do both husband and wife pull back from intimacy? As we discuss it here, it has little to do with sex. Of course, the sexual side of marriage encourages intimacy, but in most cases having sex is not the whole of true intimacy. Along with a certain level of intimacy, sex also involves passion, lust and physical satisfaction, which are not in themselves intimacy.

What is intimacy? Someone once noted that intimacy can be phonetically written as IN·TO·ME·SEE, and this is very close to the truth. Our first intimate experiences are with our mother and our father. As infants we are completely open to intimacy, particularly with our parents. Our parents are our primary role models. They are our flesh and blood. We emulate them, strive to be like them. For a baby, all things come from mother. She is Mother Earth, supplier of sustenance and nurturing. Like the earth, she never complains, and we come to expect this gracious service from her. Her role as our mother is to supply our every want and need, to nurture us and to give us everything we need or ask for. There is never a question of having to tell our mother what to do or how to do it. There is no need to argue about her role. She simply knows and does. As infants, we were trusting and open to intimacy: 'In·to·me·see.'

The neglect, abandonment or cruelty of a parent is a tremendous blow to a child. If there is no one there for him, he feels abandoned. He can't blame his mother and father—they are his role models; they can do no wrong. Instead the child internalizes the blame. He feels shame. He blames himself. "If I am abandoned, rejected, beaten, it must be my fault. Mom and Dad can't be wrong!" says the wounded psyche.

As the child grows a little older, he begins to understand, intellectually, that he is not to blame. He begins to see the defects in his parents. He begins to resent them, to resist them or to strike back at them.

In marriage, we may react strongly to little things our partner says and does, but we do not understand who it is that we are reacting against. Our true motivation is unconscious. It is as if when we were eight or nine years old and one of our parents punished us unfairly or struck us, we started hitting back, but in slow motion. Fifteen or twenty years later when we actually deliver the blow, our spouse is the one who receives its full force and fury, not our parent. And all this happens unconsciously.

If the childhood conflicts are never resolved, the pattern of fault-finding and resentment harden into a mind-set. The child also loses the ability to trust. He learns that when he needs his parents, they may not be there for him. He goes into puberty, leaves the house, goes to school, gets involved in relationships and enters marriage, trailing behind him all of these unresolved childhood hurts and distrust.

The Second Intimacy

The old feelings from childhood of distrust, lack of support and vulnerability continue in marriage, the second intimacy. The very process of sharing a bed, feelings, thoughts and beliefs with another person reawakens our original intimacy issues with our parents. Discussing things that involve opening up means being vulnerable and open to blame, criticism or even rejection. Most people will not risk this; it is too painful because it brings up old feelings. So the sacred, private area of each person's heart remains locked and guarded. We are afraid that if we allow our partner to see into us at the deepest levels, he or she will see our imperfections and stop loving us. He or she might leave us or at least use this information against us in a later argument. "If I couldn't trust my parents to be there for me, why should I trust my spouse?"

Trying to create real intimacy on top of unresolved conflicts is like painting over rust: it doesn't work. It looks fine for a while, but breakdown is happening under the surface. We must, at all costs, remove the rust. We need steel wool, the steel wool of honesty and courage and understanding. And we must rub gently—we don't want to remove the good metal. When we are finished and the metal is exposed, we must wipe it clean.

In marriage we must get rid of all rust and speak

our minds. We must separate the facts from the anger and then reveal our hurt. We still can't paint, though. There must be a primer coat consisting of words of support, understanding and gentleness. When these have been applied, we are ready for the final coat, which is our new way of relating, a fresh start unencumbered by anger, resentment or hurt. If we carry out these steps when rust appears, we will protect our marriages from decay. Rust removal sounds easy, but it is difficult and scary because it involves intimacy.

Developing True Intimacy

Another very important part of restoring harmony and developing intimacy has to do with how we see each other. Is our partner's glass of positive qualities half full or half empty?

There is an old story about two travelers who went to a wise man for advice. The first one asked, "Is this a bad day to begin my journey across the desert?" The sage responded, "Yes, it is indeed a bad day. You should not go."

The second traveler went to the sage and asked, "Is this a good day to begin my journey?" The sage answered, "Yes, this is a good day. You should proceed."

When the two travelers compared notes after meeting with the sage, they were confused by the conflicting advice. Together, they returned to the sage for an explanation. He told them, "As you see something, so it will be." The sage turned to the first traveler. "Because you felt uneasy and fearful, bad things would have taken place on your trip."

To the second traveler he said, "Your heart is open, and you are thinking good thoughts. Your trip will be beautiful if you start out in this positive state of mind." He went on to tell the two men the importance of seeing things in a positive light. How we greet the day can determine in large part how the day progresses. How we view our partner can determine in large part how our marriage progresses.

If we focus primarily on our partner's faults, it gets harder and harder to see any good qualities. It's like placing a red filter in front of your eyes: everything you see is red. On the other hand, if we see that our partner is fundamentally a good person in spite of certain imperfections or failings, then his or her actions and words are much more likely to radiate understanding and gentleness. At a deeper level, if we know in our hearts that the true nature of our partner is good and that the lower nature simply obscures this good, it will help us focus on the positive and forgive the faults. When the great sage Bawa Muhaiyaddeen addressed his students, he always began by saying, "Jeweled lights of my eyes," for this is what he saw. He looked through the imperfections and saw the light in each person.

Visualize an uncut diamond. To the untrained eye, it looks like an ugly stone with many defects on the surface, misshapen and dull. Yet a jeweler holding it in his skilled hands treasures it, for he sees its intrinsic value. He sees the light emanating from the depths of the stone. He begins his work of cutting, grinding, faceting and polishing until the stone reflects its true perfection and value. Good parents readily do this with an ungainly and insecure child. They know that focusing on the good in the child and nourishing him with good qualities will enable a beautiful person to emerge, reflecting what he has been shown and taught.

This is how a husband and wife must treat each other. The physical beauty that originally attracted us may fade, but we saw a spiritual beauty as well. Moving forward in the relationship, we must reach this plane so that we focus on the gem inherent in each other. It has far greater value than the glitter of less valuable gems. It is a pearl of great price, but it takes time, attention and effort to extract it from its depths.

Developing intimacy requires even more work and trust and patience, but it is worth it. The risks should be taken in little pieces and at the right time, when both of you are very relaxed, such as during 'pillow talk' or when the children are gone, or when you are not enmeshed in duties and responsibilities.

If it seems there is just no alone time, you will have to make the time. You might set aside one night a week, get a babysitter and go out for dinner. If grandparents are nearby, leave the children for a weekend. Do whatever is needed to establish a calm period of aloneness together where there can be a positive focus, without fear, on resolving problems and building trust.

Some couples may choose to consult a marriage counselor. If the counselor is wise and trustworthy, much can be done in the 'safe' time spent each week in the counselor's office. Each person must come to see that the imagined threat of intimacy with its roots in childhood is much more illusory than real.

I have heard it said that in a good marriage each partner tries to heal the other's childhood wounds and fails, but in the process there is support, nourishment and understanding of one another. Love and respect begin to blossom.

I hear, I forget,
I see, I remember,
I do, I understand.

—AUTHOR UNKNOWN

Doing Is Understanding

To paraphrase a truth we all have heard many times, it is not what you are given in life but how you deal with it that counts. You can listen to countless words of wisdom or read a thousand books, but unless you put what you have heard and seen into practice, it counts for very little. For example, when one person in a marriage is ill-tempered and fault-finding, the other has a choice: he or she can either lash back or can quietly, usually with great internal struggle, practice tolerance and patience. These efforts have nothing to do with whether the other person is bad or good. Your focus must be on developing your own good qualities and eliminating the bad ones. It really has to be *goodness done only for the sake of goodness.* If you can take these words into your heart and do your best to put them into practice, you will come to understand.

The battle of the sexes is perhaps the most sensitive and troublesome issue in a marriage, and it is one that is rarely dealt with openly and frankly. It is a tremendous barrier to trust and intimacy, and an important opportunity to do goodness only for the sake of goodness.

When we marry, the primeval duties of mother are already embedded in our psyches. A woman's role as nurturer and provider of sustenance is part of our deepest memory. Women do, of course, provide this kind of love and care to their children. What is interesting is that we husbands instinctively, albeit unknowingly, expect the nurturing atmosphere our mothers provided to continue into marriage. Although we are supposed to be partners in a marriage, the child part of us asserts itself. 'Mama' should do everything: take care of the house, feed the kids, clean up the messes and, lest we forget, also devote full energy to us in the wife aspect of her role. The age-old double standard asserts itself. We have our duties and our wives have their duties, but it turns out that our wives have double duties. In our view, our wives are supposed to take care of us and nourish us as if we were still babies. Nothing we ask for should be too much.

We are very capable of doing many of the duties our wives take on, but it is just a lot easier to let them be done for us. We husbands need to face the fact that the part of a woman's psyche that longs to provide nourishment for a child should not have to stretch to provide in like manner for her husband. In many marriages, this imbalance must be corrected before harmony and intimacy can be restored.

We need to look at ourselves honestly, see our transference of dependency and try to correct it. As long as we continue to project our dependency needs on our wives, we will not be able to grow and assume our share of emotional responsibility in the household. Men must come to understand fully the necessity for shared duties. They need to understand the burdens they place on their wives with their conscious and unconscious demands. The truth becomes quite evident when a woman is raising children. A baby demands her energies and her nurturing qualities fulltime, and no matter how accustomed her husband is to getting what he wants when he wants it, he can no longer count on her to nourish him in the same way. She has become the true mother to the true dependent, and not to the impersonator. What is required on the part of the husband at this time is understanding, patience and compassion. If he can exercise these good qualities, there will be harmony. Otherwise, jealousy, resentment and self-pity will creep into his mind and cause no end of trouble.

On the other hand, women can use their many God-given qualities to maintain harmony in the home. The abundance of understanding, compassion, love and tenderness that help them bear and nurture children make women natural peacemakers, and a wise woman will use her gifts to restore peace when conflict arises.

For example, women are often faced with a spouse who exhibits the traits of a petulant child. At this critical flashpoint, patience, understanding and tolerance can save the day. This is not the time for a woman to tell her husband about transference of dependency! She must calm him just as she would calm a petulant or fearful child. Later on, when his fire has gone out, they can discuss the situation more objectively. Trying to reason with a man who is upset is like talking to a hungry person instead of bringing food.

Timing is very important in sorting out problems. Remember, even an adult needs to be soothed like a child sometimes. If a woman can understand that and use her gifts without resentment, a couple can make great progress toward a more harmonious life.

One thing is certain: once we begin to intellectualize or justify or fault-find, we are finished. Everybody loses, no matter who 'wins.' The focal point of the struggle ceases to be in ourselves and comes down to the level of fighting with our spouse.

There is another crucial but very subtle area that provides us a tremendous opportunity to find more peace in marriage — the little things.

The many little tasks we do on a daily basis — the way we wash dishes, set a table, clean the house, keep a garden or drive a car — are based on habit patterns we have developed throughout the course of our lives. The way we do these little things is second nature by the time we marry and conveys our distinctive style and flavor. Left to ourselves, we do them efficiently, and the same is true of our partner.

Doing good only for the sake of goodness is a real challenge to our established habit patterns. We are accustomed to doing things our way, and moreover, we think our own way is the best way. It is time-proven and comfortable. Suddenly we are faced with our partner's very different methods, and our partner is faced with ours. We discover with some alarm that our partner does many of these things *the wrong way!*

What happens? We interrupt our partner, criticize and give 'helpful' directions on the proper way to do the task. We all know by now that if this persists, there will be an argument. This is really evident in driving because safety is an issue, and we all have a tendency to think our way of driving is the safest. Obviously, this adds fuel to the arrogance of our criticism. We see that our partner is driving too fast or too slowly, takes curves the 'wrong' way and brakes and parks the 'wrong' way. Couples argue over using a map versus asking directions or going on intuition.

It is the same with conversation. We may view a person or a political, spiritual or emotional issue in very different ways. How often do we find ourselves irritated and even angry when our partner interrupts with criticism or unnecessary disagreement?

The devil is in the details, the small things. When

we dig in our heels and focus on winning instead of focusing on the good of the relationship, disagreement becomes argument, which is likely to turn to anger, and with anger the moment is lost and maybe even the day. If grace is present, we may be able to accept the disagreement as a spiritual exercise and surrender our way of doing something. This doesn't mean we have to abandon a sense of our own validity. It simply means that we may choose to acquiesce in order to promote harmony at a sticky point in our interaction. Troublesome matters can be discussed when there is more openness, perhaps during pillow talk.

The little things in life offer a good barometer as to how flexible and surrendered we are, and we can use them as guideposts to our progress. Couples who can adapt and be tolerant about each other's viewpoints and driving habits and cleaning methods are more apt to have a higher overall degree of unity in their marriage.

When we can focus on controlling our impatience and anger over the little things in marriage, we will have accomplished a substantial goal.

True marriage comes from the qualities of the heart. No matter what the outward difference, when these qualities match in each heart, it is a good marriage. For the qualities of true love are qualities born of good behavior and good actions. These qualities will nurture patience, contentment, trust and praise of God in each soul and create paradise on earth. In a good marriage, tolerance, patience, kindness, considering the other's life as one's own life, justice, peacefulness and unity must overcome all separations and conflicts, all differences and sorrows.

—M. R. BAWA MUHAIYADDEEN

The True Marriage

⟨❧⟩

Wise teachers in ancient times have said that marriage is half the *deen*. *Deen* can be translated as the light, the soul, or the understanding of our true nature, so we might say that marriage can provide us with half the understanding of our true nature. Another way of putting it is that marriage is half the work of getting into Heaven.

How each partner treats the other is the most accurate reflection of character and prayer. And the greatest prayers we can offer are not necessarily done on our knees; they are done in service to the other through acts of compassion, understanding and love. And it is precisely by transcending the lower nature and nourishing the higher one that we stand tall. For the young adult entering into marriage, these truths may come as a shock, even though they are part of many marriage ceremonies.

Corinthians I - XIII is a Bible verse often used in marriage ceremonies:

> *Love is patient and kind; love is not jealous or boastful; it is not arrogant or rude. Love does*

not insist on its own way; it is not irritable or resentful; it does not rejoice at wrong, but rejoices in the right. Love bears all things, believes all things, hopes all things, endures all things.

Unfortunately, I suspect that seldom do the partners truly understand that these words are not ornamental; they are indeed the very bricks and mortar of a successful union. Or, to build upon William Shakespeare:

To err is human, to forgive is divine.
What is divine is Godlike.
What is Godlike gives peace and
  understanding.
And all of this takes time.

When we touch our center, the light, our true being—through prayer or a realization or an affirmation from someone or a spontaneous opening of the heart—nothing can negatively affect this state. A negative comment or a difficulty in a relationship will be dealt with calmly and with equanimity. We cannot be shaken when that connection to our inner being, the truth, is there.

To go back to our garden analogy, God has placed in the garden of our being many valuable seeds. Among them are all varieties of delicious and nourishing fruits and vegetables and even some rare and exotic plants whose taste and scent are heavenly. God also created thousands of seeds that grow into weeds; so many, in fact, that they vastly outnumber the useful plants. He has also given us the tools and knowledge to nurture our inner garden and to pull out the destructive plants. Daily maintenance is vital to keep the weeds from smothering the useful plants, ruining the harvest and depriving us of our God-given opportunity to taste the special fruits destined for us. These are fruits of knowledge and wisdom, and they can only be cultivated and experienced while we are here in this world.

There is absolutely no use in worrying about someone else's weeds when our own garden is overrun with weeds of its own. To put it another way, as I stated emphatically before, we cannot change anyone else, we can only change ourselves. Many years ago, I had a powerful experience while running a therapy group in my clinic in Baltimore. The group was composed of eight women, all wives or companions of alcoholic men. Some of the men were 'recovering' and had stopped drinking, but others had not. Every woman in the group was faced with a huge gap between what she wanted or needed and what she was getting.

The women researched this problem for months. Each week they shared their pain, anger and frustration as they questioned their relationships and searched for the proper and wisest ways to respond to their situations. All loved their partners, but not what their partners did and said. Gradually they worked out an answer that they all agreed was correct and wise. They allowed themselves the right to leave their marriages, but with one proviso: that before they left they would clear up their own personal character defects. They felt that once they had eliminated their retaliatory reactions, they would be free to leave peacefully and without anger.

In the end, *not one of the women left her relationship*. Once the women had established a sense of peace in themselves, what their spouses did no longer affected them so intensely. They found they were able to live quite peacefully in spite of the difficulties they were still encountering. Armed with this new sense of equipoise, they chose to continue in their marriages. In several cases, their newfound sense of stability was so strong that the spouses were positively affected and were motivated to work on changing themselves. Even the women who did not succeed in changing themselves as fully as they had envisioned came to understand the spiritual power they gained in the process and did not want to stop working on themselves. Hence, they too stayed in their marriages.

Once honest work begins, we sense the potential in ourselves. We come to know that peace lies within, not in winning the fight with our spouse or changing our circumstances. This recognition is most important and lies at the heart of a successful marriage. In

Alcoholics Anonymous' Big Book, Bill Wilson writes:

> *I am beginning to see that all my troubles have their root in a habitual and absolute dependence upon my personal prestige, security, and romantic attachment. When these things go wrong there is depression. Now this absolute dependence upon people and situations for emotional security is, I think, the immense and devastating fallacy that makes us miserable.*
>
> *This craving for such dependencies, this utter dependence upon people and situations can only lead to conflict, both on the surface and at depth. We are making demands on circumstances and people that are bound to fail us. The only safe and sure channel of absolute dependence is upon God Himself.*

When we finally come to realize the peace that arises out of taking responsibility for ourselves, we will see a way out of our misery. There is a tiny dot inside each of us, much like a fetus longing to be nourished and to grow. This tiny dot is wisdom and peace. It is the soul, it is goodness, and it is our true nature. It is fed by practicing the Godly qualities of patience, tolerance, forgiveness, understanding, compassion and love. As we bring these qualities into our actions, we literally strip away the bad qualities that obscure our real nature. It is like scratching away the varnish on a bulb so that the light can shine through with greater brilliance. We can have experiences of peace more and more frequently, experiences of peace that deepen and become part of our very being. The fetus grows. We experience gratitude to God. We understand the power of goodness. We start to understand how it feels to have a 'melting heart.'

If we can continue this process and not be discouraged by setbacks, we will reach our goal. This is what it means to *see the truth as goodness and put this goodness into action*. The purpose and meaning of our lives begin to emerge. *To serve others with a melting heart is our true purpose.* This is the reason we are alive. The more we understand, the more we come to see our marriages in a different light. The 'I' versus 'you' changes into 'we.' Unity replaces self-business and the struggle for control. No longer do we feel we need to change our partners. No longer do we depend upon externals for our happiness. Finally, we understand that we have inside us everything we need, and that it was always there. We are sufficient unto ourselves, and out of this completeness we can give to our partners and our families deep and pure understanding. From that place, we will see that marriage has become a true garden of Eden.

> *If you practice patience, you become more patient.*
> *If you become more patient, you become quieter.*
> *If you become quieter, you become more aware.*

If you become more aware, you become more
  compassionate.
If you become more compassionate, you become
  more understanding.
If you become more understanding, you become wiser.
If you become wiser, you become more accepting.
If you become more accepting, you become more
  peaceful.
If you become more peaceful, you see unity in all
  things.
If you see unity in all things, you become more
  grateful.
If you become more grateful, you thank God.
If you thank God, you will praise God.
If you praise God, you have understood Life and the
  meaning of your life,
And you have come to know that the Kingdom of
  Heaven is indeed within.

Recipes for the True Marriage

THE POT AND THE LID
by M. R. Bawa Muhaiyaddeen

A pot to fit the lid
A lid to fit the pot

When people see a close married couple they say, "This pair is like a pot and a lid." The connection between husband and wife should be like this. Pots vary in size and shape; the middle may be wide and the bottom narrow. But no matter what the shape of the pot, the lid must fit the mouth of the pot.

When we cook food, the heat, weight, and pressure are felt by the pot. The whole weight is in the pot, not the lid. The lid is the man, and the pot is the woman. When the pot suffers with the heat, and the food in the pot boils up, the lid will lift. At that point, instead of complaining about the minor difficulty he is undergoing, the man must realize the weight, suffering and pain felt by the woman, who bears the burden of the family.

The lid must be lifted when the pot boils and the

contents stirred with a spoon to ease the heat and keep the food from boiling over into the fire. Only then will there be food to satisfy hunger.

The woman bears the family's burdens, sorrows, mental depressions and physical illnesses. When she begins to boil with all the difficulties and sufferings, the man should lift up the lid and stir with the spoon of wisdom to keep the pot from boiling over. When she comes to talk to her husband, he must comfort her with wisdom and love by listening to her complaints, thereby easing the boiling heat within her and giving her peace. As the spoon was used to stir the pot, a husband must use his wisdom and love to ease the mounting sorrows of his wife, thereby maintaining the unity of the pot and the lid. If he continues to stir, releasing the heat, there will be unity. If he does not, a heart filled with mounting suffering will break with the excess pressure, and the unity of their life together will be destroyed.

Men must think of this with wisdom and give love and comfort to their wives, who bear so much suffering and trouble in life.

A wife must be able to bear burdens. Everything that a man brings is a burden. Everything he gives her is a burden. If he has a fight at work, he will come and unload that burden on her. If there are any problems in his relationships, he brings these burdens and lays them on her. So he will come and unload both good and bad burdens. He might also bring hastiness, anger, or impatience. So with patience she should be tolerant. She should look at his face and realize what state he is in.

She shouldn't try to advise him about the burdens that he brings in because then he will only bring her another one. So she has to think about this. That is not the time to tell him and advise him. She must first make him peaceful. There is a pillow mantra. That is the time when she must be able to advise him as to what his problems are. She can't do it when he first arrives home. So whatever may come, her duty is to see it and make it peaceful and unload those burdens so that the qualities of God, the belief in God, the good actions of God will prevail. Both hearts should be entwined and both duties should intermingle. Although the bodies may be two and separate, both lives must be like one. If the husband is ill, she is ill. If the husband is happy, the wife should be happy. If the wife is happy, the husband should be happy. If the wife is ill, the husband should feel that illness.

She must speak with patience and contentment. That is the highest of the qualities of a wife, to speak with patience and with tenderness. If she only looks at the husband with these qualities, the moment he sees her he will be gentle. She must always treat him like a bridegroom. Her qualities will make him strong. Even more than her beauty, it is her love, her compassion, and her tenderness that will hold him tight so that he does not want to leave her. These beautiful qualities are the magnetic current that she has. Both partners must display loving words, soothing words, beauty, love, and compassion. If they utilize these, what is there that we cannot correct? What is there that we cannot control? What is there that they cannot correct? What is there that they cannot control? What is there that they cannot tame? They will be able to bring under their will everything in the entire universe. We must think of this.*

~

* *M. R. Bawa Muhaiyaddeen, Questions of Life–Answers of Wisdom*

Ingredients for the True Marriage

1. Never both be angry at once.
2. Never yell at each other unless the house is on fire.
3. Yield to the wishes of the other as an exercise in self-discipline if you can't think of a better reason.
4. If you have a choice between making yourself or your mate look good, choose your mate.
5. If you feel you must criticize, do so lovingly.
6. Never bring up a mistake of the past. Your silence will be greatly appreciated.
7. Neglect the whole world rather than each other.
8. Never let the day end without saying at least one complimentary thing to your life's partner.
9. Never meet without an affectionate greeting.
10. When you've said or done something hurtful, acknowledge it and ask for forgiveness.
11. Remember, it takes two to get an argument going. Invariably, the one who is wrong is the one who will be doing most of the talking.
12. Never go to bed angry.

—AUTHOR UNKNOWN

Recommended Reading

Questions of Life—Answers of Wisdom, Vol. 1 & 2
The Golden Words of a Sufi Sheikh
To Die Before Death—The Sufi Way of Life

These books and others are available at:

The Bawa Muhaiyaddeen Fellowship
5820 Overbrook Avenue
Philadelphia, PA 19131
215-879-6300
www.bmf.org